Living in
SCOTLAND

Annabelle Lynch

W
FRANKLIN WATTS
LONDON · SYDNEY

First published in 2014 by
Franklin Watts
338 Euston Road
London
NW1 3BH

Franklin Watts Australia
Level 17/207 Kent Street
Sydney
NSW 2000

HB ISBN 978 1 4451 2795 8
Library ebook ISBN 978 1 4451 2799 6

Dewey number: 941.1'08612
A CIP catalogue record for this book is
available from the British Library.

Series Editor: Julia Bird
Series Design: D.R. ink

Picture credits: Abimages/Dreamstime: 14b. Alamy: 17tl. Steve Allen/Dreamstime: 21br. Allstar PL/Alamy: 17b. Alvera/Dreamstime: 18t. D Beaston/Dreamstime: 11b. Noel Bennett/istockphoto: 8b. Bob Brookfield/Dreamstime: 7t. Valeria Cantone/Dreamstime: 21bl. Ron Chapple/Dreamstime: 8t. Chime and Sense/Dreamstime: 12t. Paul Cowan/Dreamstime: 15cl. Fasphotographic/Dreamstime: 17cr. Fintasique/Dreamstime: 6b. Karl Franz/Dreamstime: 13c. Tatiana Gladskikh/Shutterstock: front cover tcr. Global stock/istockphoto: 4t. idscott/istockphoto: 5t. Emmano Iselle/Dreamstime: 21t. pks1/Dreamstime: 13b. Gina Kelly/Alamy: 19t. Judy Kennamer/Dreamstime: 6t. Lagartija/Dreamstime: 7b. Charlotte Leaper/Dreamstime: 18b. Stephen Meese/Dreamstime: 11t. modern image 84/istockphoto: 5b. Sergey Novikov/Shutterstock: front cover tl. onfilm/istockphoto: 9b. Colin Palmer Photography/Alamy: 13t. Geoff Pickering/Dreamstime: 10b. pio3/Shutterstock: front cover tcl. Norman Pogson/Dreamstime: 20b. Luca Quadrio/Dreamstime: 12b. Andres Rodriguez/Dreamstime: 20t. Shalith/Shutterstock: front cover b, 9t. Darren Sharvey/Dreamstime: 16b. Shestakoff/Shutterstock: front cover tlc. Dmitry Shironev/Dreamstime: 16t. Stockcube/Dreamstime: 19b. 2xSamara.com/Shutterstock: front cover tr. Olga Voronishcheva/Dreamstime: 10t. Whiteboxmedia/Alamy: 15tr. Darren Wise/istockphoto: 14t. Zurijeta/Dreamstime: 9c. Zurijeta/Shutterstock: front cover trc.

Printed in China

Franklin Watts is a division of
Hachette Children's Books,
an Hachette UK company.
www.hachette.co.uk

Contents

Words in bold are in the glossary on page 23.

Welcome to Scotland

Hello! I live in Scotland. It is one of the four countries of the United Kingdom.

Scotland in the UK

Scotland is the furthest north of all the countries in the UK. It shares a long **border** with England in the south.

Shetland

Orkneys

Atlantic Ocean

North Sea

Hebrides

Highlands

Cairngorms

Grampians

Aberdeen

Ben Nevis

Glasgow

EDINBURGH

SCOTLAND

NORTHERN IRELAND

ENGLAND

WALES

High or low?

In the south of Scotland, there are lots of hills and **moors**. The Highlands are in the north. They are very **mountainous**. In the middle of Scotland, the land is flat and good for farming. Most of Scotland's cities are found there.

Rolling hills and moors are found in the south of Scotland.

Cool place

The weather in Scotland can be colder than in the rest of the UK because it is further north. In winter, it often snows, especially in the mountains.

People in Scotland

I come from Scotland. People who come from Scotland are called Scottish.

Around the world

Around 5.2 million people live in Scotland today. Most people who live here were born in Scotland, but some people have **immigrated** to live here from other countries, such as India and China. Scottish people have also **settled** in countries as far away as Canada and New Zealand.

Red hot!
....
More people in Scotland have red hair than in any country in the world.

Where people live

Most people live in the middle of Scotland, in or near the big cities of Glasgow and Edinburgh (see pages 8–9). Fewer people live in the Highlands and in Scotland's many islands (see pages 12–13).

Religion →

Christianity is the biggest religion in Scotland. Around 16 per cent of Christians in Scotland are **Roman Catholics**. Many people don't follow any religion.

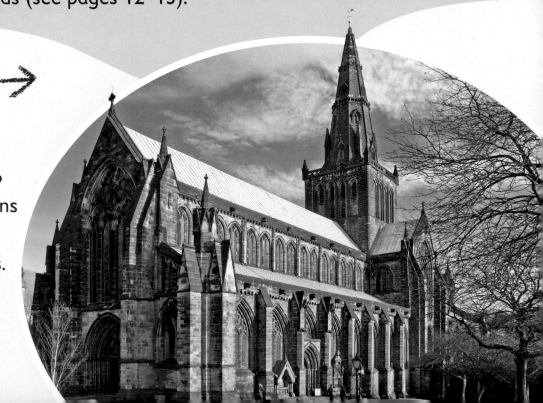

Cities

I live in a city called Glasgow. People who come from Glasgow are known as Glaswegians.

New buildings next to the River Clyde in Glasgow.

Big business

Glasgow is the biggest city in Scotland and the third biggest city in the UK. Lots of people come here to work. It used to be an important **port** and a centre for building ships. Today, most people work in banking and other businesses such as **engineering**.

Old town

Edinburgh is the **capital** city of Scotland. It is also the centre of **government**. Many banks and businesses are found here, but there are also lots of **museums** and other old buildings. Millions of tourists come to Edinburgh every year to visit them.

An oil platform in the North Sea.

Fish for oil

Aberdeen is on the east coast of Scotland, next to the North Sea. It has an important oil industry that brings lots of jobs to the town. It is also a big fishing port.

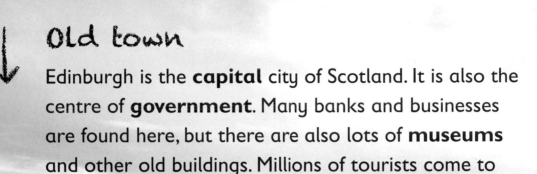

Countryside

I live in the Highlands. It is very beautiful here. Lots of people visit the Highlands to go climbing and to take in the amazing views.

Mountains

The biggest mountains in the UK are found in Scotland, including **ranges** of mountains such as the Grampians and the Cairngorms. The UK's highest mountain, Ben Nevis, is found in the Grampians. At the top, it can snow even in the middle of summer!

Up in the air

Ben Nevis is 1,344 metres high.

Lochs

In Scotland, lakes and sea **inlets** are called lochs. There are more than 30,000 lochs scattered across Scotland. The biggest loch is Loch Ness (see page 19).

Loch Lomond lies between central Scotland and the Highlands.

Wildlife →

Scotland is home to lots of wildlife, including the rare red squirrel, wild goats and pine martens. Birds such as eagles and kingfishers fly above the lochs, while red grouse and the capercaillie hide in the forests.

Pine marten

Coast and islands

*I live by the **coast**. Scotland's coast is surrounded by hundreds of islands. Some are big. Others are really tiny!*

By the sea

Scotland's coastline stretches for thousands of kilometres. Along it, you can find long, sandy beaches, rocky cliffs and hidden **coves**. The west coast is warmer and wetter than the east coast.

Island language

Lots of people living on the islands speak an old Scottish language called Gaelic.

Beautiful Luskentyre Beach is found in the Outer Hebrides.

Island life

There are around 800 islands off Scotland's coast. They are in groups of islands called the Orkneys, the Shetland Islands and the Inner and Outer Hebrides. Only about 95 of the islands are **inhabited**.

The island of Barra has a funny airport – the beach!

Watery home

Lots of wildlife live in or near Scotland's seas. Big **colonies** of puffins and guillemots nest among the high, rocky cliffs. Grey seals, bottlenose dolphins and minke and killer whales swim in the cool water.

Bottlenose dolphins

Puffins

What we eat

We eat lots of the same foods in Scotland as in the rest of the UK. Some are special to Scotland, though.

Porridge

A favourite breakfast in Scotland is porridge. It is made with oats and milk or water. You can add fruit, jam, salt or syrup to it, or just eat it as it is. Yum!

Oats grow well in Scotland. They can be used to make porridge.

Fishy foods

We eat lots of seafood in Scotland. Arbroath smokies are a famous type of smoked fish. Cullen skink is a tasty soup made with smoked haddock, potato and onion. And of course, we all love fish and chips.

Have some haggis?

One traditional Scottish dish is called haggis. It is **minced** sheep lungs, heart and liver, mixed with onion and oatmeal, and cooked in the sheep's stomach or a sausage skin. It sounds strange, but it is really delicious!

A wee drink

Scottish whisky is the most famous whisky in the world. One bottle once sold for more than £300,000!

SCOTTISH WHISKY £300,000

Having fun

Scotland is a great place to have fun! There is a lot to do outdoors. We also love playing and watching sport.

Fresh air fun ↑

In summer, we head to the countryside to go cycling, walking and camping. In winter, you can go skiing high up in the snowy mountains.

Skiing fun in Aviemore in the Cairngorms.

By the water ↑

You can go fishing or canoeing
on some of Scotland's many lochs
and rivers all year round. At the
seaside, you can go surfing
or sailing or just have fun
on the beach.

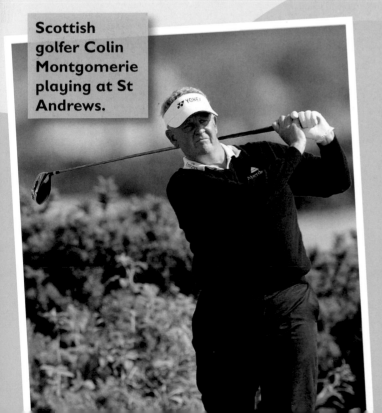

Scottish golfer Colin Montgomerie playing at St Andrews.

Sports

Scotland is the home of golf. Every
few years, the world's top golfers
play in a famous **tournament**
called the Open at St Andrews
on the east coast. We also love
playing and watching football
and rugby.

Famous places

There are lots of interesting and beautiful places to visit in Scotland, both old and new.

Island castle

Eilean Donan Castle is one of the most beautiful castles in the world. It is found on an island on Loch Dornie in the Highlands. It was first built over 800 years ago for King Alexander II of Scotland. Today, you can explore it for yourself.

Lake lady

The Loch Ness monster is also known as Nessie!

The Loch Ness monster might look like this.

Lake monster

Loch Ness in the Highlands is famous around the world. Over the years, people say they have seen a huge monster swimming in the loch. Lots of people visit the loch to try to see it for themselves, but no one knows if it really exists!

Spin around →

The Falkirk Wheel was built to link two **canals** that run between Edinburgh and Glasgow. It can lift up to eight boats at a time and moves them between the two canals, spinning as it goes. It is a thrilling ride!

Festivals

We celebrate lots of the same festivals in Scotland as the rest of the UK, such as Christmas and Diwali. Some are special to Scotland, though.

Burns Night

On 25 January every year we celebrate Scotland's most famous **poet**, Robert Burns. We eat a meal of haggis, mashed potatoes and turnips, and read some of Burns' most famous poems aloud.

Summer fun

Every summer, there is a big festival in Edinburgh. There is music, dance, theatre and comedy. Millions of people come to Edinburgh both to watch and take part.

Highland Games

Every August, the Highland Gathering is held in Argyll. There are traditional Scottish games, such as the caber toss (see right), Scottish music, such as the bagpipes, and dancing.

Tossing the caber means throwing a long, heavy pole as far as you can. It is believed to have come from people throwing logs across narrow valleys.

Scotland: Fast facts

Capital: Edinburgh

Population: 5,313,600 (2011)

Area: 78,387 km²

Official language: English

Currency: Pound sterling

Main religions: Christianity (Church of Scotland), Roman Catholicism

Longest river: River Tay (188 km)

Highest mountain: Ben Nevis (1,344 m)

National holidays: New Year (1 & 2 January) Good Friday, Easter Sunday, first Monday in May, last Monday in May, first Monday in August, St Andrew's Day (30 November), Christmas Day (25 December), Boxing Day (26 December)

Glossary

border a line that divides two countries

canal a long, narrow stretch of water built for boats to travel on

capital the city in which the government of a country meets

coast where the land meets the sea

colony a group of animals living together in a place

cove a small bay on the coast

engineering the industry of building and looking after machines

government the group of people who run a country

immigrate to move to live in a different country

inhabited lived in

inlet a narrow stretch of water between the land and a lake or the sea

minced very finely chopped

moor an area of high, open land covered with rough grass

mountainous an area where there are lots of mountains

museum a place where old, interesting and beautiful things are kept

poet someone who writes poems

port a place by the sea from where boats and ships arrive and depart

range a group

Roman Catholic a member of a branch of the Christian Church of which the Pope is the head

settle to live in a place

tournament a sporting competition

Index